How I Feel

# I Feel Angry

By Connor Stratton

**www.littlebluehousebooks.com**

Little Blue House is distributed by North Star Editions:
sales@northstareditions.com | 888-417-0195

Produced for Little Blue House by Red Line Editorial.

Photographs ©: Shutterstock Images, cover, 4, 9, 10–11, 15, 16–17, 18, 20–21, 23, 24 (top left); iStockphoto, 6–7, 12, 24 (top right), 24 (bottom left), 24 (bottom right)

**Library of Congress Control Number: 2020913842**

**ISBN**
978-1-64619-294-6 (hardcover)
978-1-64619-312-7 (paperback)
978-1-64619-348-6 (ebook pdf)
978-1-64619-330-1 (hosted ebook)

Printed in the United States of America
Mankato, MN
012021

## About the Author

Connor Stratton enjoys writing books for children and watching movies, such as *Inside Out*. He's always trying to understand his feelings better. He lives in Minnesota.

# Table of Contents

# Why I'm Angry

Sometimes I feel angry.
My sister won't share
with me, and that's
why I'm angry.

My brother pushed me, and that's why I'm angry.

I didn't get a treat, and that's why I'm angry.

treat

We left the park, and that's why I'm angry. It's not fun to feel angry.

park

11

# What I Do

I do different things
when I'm angry.
I feel angry, so I
make a frown.

I feel angry, so I cross my arms.

I feel angry, so I yell.

It's okay to feel angry.

# Feeling Better

I tell my dad.

I tell him I feel angry.

I tell my mom.

My mom hugs me.

She holds me tight.

I take deep breaths and count to ten.

I feel better now.

# Glossary

arms

park

frown

treats

# Index